Heresy

www.lulu.com

Published by Lulu.
ISBN: 978-1-4710-2337-8

CONTENTS

1. THE DELIBERATE MISINTERPRETATION OF THE CONSTITUTION OF THE UNITED KINGDOM.

The constitution of the United Kingdom ,which is the Christian principles ,civil rights , acknowledges the existence and the dangers of supernatural powers and senses , and forbids the misuse of these supernatural powers and senses to harm mentally or physically the civilized or to breach the peace in a civilized society .But the unlawful interpretation of the constitution of the United Kingdom , by the uncivilized with supernatural powers and senses, claims that the constitution gives them the permission to kill , make people ill , cause accidents ,age people ,cause environmental disasters like earthquakes ,floods ,thunderstorm ,insecurity ,famine etc. After all this, the uncivilized also claim that from their unlawful interpretation of the constitution ,after you have been killed by them , they will resurrect you then decide if you were good or bad . If it is decided by them that you have been good, they will send you to their idea of heaven .If it is decided by them that you have been bad; they will send you to their idea of hell. This is all after they have unlawfully killed you or allowed you to die themselves. Apart from their uncivilized nature interfering with their judgements about what constitutes heaven, their interpretation of the constitution is treasonous. Their idea of what constitutes heaven and hell are both hell .According to the correct interpretation of the constitution of the United Kingdom , death ,ageing ,illness are punishments meant for the uncivilized that misuse their supernatural powers and senses to harm mentally or physically the civilized or to breach the peace in a civilized society. You cannot kill someone unlawfully or kill them as a punishment, to then resurrect them to judge their past deeds to decide, whether they should go to heaven or whether they should go to hell. I can only conclude that the intention of the uncivilized , given the unlawful , interpretation of the constitution of the United Kingdom, which includes misusing their supernatural powers and senses to mislead people into eating meat , fish ,eggs contrary to the guidance of the constitution , is that they intend to create hell on earth. According to the history of the United Kingdom, regarding, the interpretation and application of the Christian principles (the constitution of the United Kingdom), those that were misusing supernatural powers and senses to harm mentally or physically the civilized (those without supernatural powers and senses), or to breach the peace in a civilized society, were accused of practicing witchcraft, and were punished by being burnt while still alive. The way round the problem for the uncivilized (those with supernatural powers and senses), that wanted to continue misusing their supernatural powers and senses (witchcraft) to harm mentally or physically the civilized (those without supernatural powers and senses) or to breach the peace in a civilized society, was to take over the running of the country, and to implement their own unlawful, interpretation and application of the constitution of the United Kingdom. This illegal interpretation and application of the constitution of the United Kingdom, allows them to openly practice witchcraft (the misuse of supernatural powers and senses) to harm mentally and physically the civilized and to breach the peace constantly in civilized society. The problem the uncivilized keep on encountering with their open disregard for the sacred instructions of the constitution of the United Kingdom , is that the constitution ,the Christian principles is civil rights ,and these civil rights are sacred rights .To violate these sacred rights is different from the fights amongst the uncivilized. Their misjudgement regarding these sacred rights originates from the uncivilized pretending to be civilized, and think that the violations of these rights amongst themselves while pretending to be of a civilized nature, is actually the same as violating the rights of someone of a real civilized nature. These civil rights are sacred rights when it involves someone of a real civilized nature , and when the uncivilized misuse their supernatural powers and senses to violate these sacred rights , they are going to be severely punished, according to the instructions of the correct interpretation of the guidance of the constitution of the United Kingdom. The prospect of life surrounded by this level of wickedness is daunting, impossible to comprehend, which makes it easy to give in to the conspiracy of the uncivilized that have deliberately set out to misuse their supernatural powers and senses to create hell on earth. According to the constitution, the only way to overcome this serious problem is to interpret and apply the instructions of the guidance of the constitution correctly .We have to live peacefully together, and eliminate any form of wickedness amongst the inhabitants of this planet. The young are easily initiated into these current unlawful practices because they believe they have no choice. Who can the young complain to , when the government are those illegally governing and openly practicing and encouraging openly the misuse of supernatural powers and senses to harm mentally or physically the civilized , the vulnerable and to breach the peace in a civilized society. The unprotected status of the uncivilized, regardless of race, gender, age makes complaining suicidal. The protection of the uncivilized are linked to the sacred rights of the civilized. This means that the constitution of the United Kingdom, the Christian principles, civil rights, has to be identified, interpreted, and applied correctly. The civilized have to be confirmed or acknowledged as having dominion over this planet, according to the guidance of the constitution. It is not enough for the uncivilized to pretend to be civilized .You must be of a civilized nature to fulfil the sacred requirements of the constitution of the United Kingdom. Another way that the uncivilized try to compromise the civil nature of the civilized, is when they want to make you believe that your rejection of their abusive, unlawful actions, means that the civilized need to loosen up, or need to toughen up. And the only way that the civilized will accept such horrific , unlawful practices , is to have our civil nature compromised , in order to undermine our civil rights , and make it easier for the uncivilized to create hell on earth. The misconception of the intellect of the civilized was borne from the conspiracy of the uncivilized, to compromise our only authorized source of knowledge, education. This compromise of our only source of knowledge was achieved by the collective participation of the uncivilized, with misinformation and misleading practices. There are decisions that no one is allowed to make for someone else. These decisions includes the decisions about life and death , access to goods and services in the guise of politics ,discomforts arising from illnesses ,ageing , physical alterations etc. In order to continue with the unlawful practices of making decisions for other people, they build up a culture of dependency, by misusing their supernatural powers and senses .The culture of dependency is achieved by interfering with your self- confidence by the misuse of their supernatural powers and senses. The uncivilized approach the civilized as if the civilized are meant to do the impossible and supernaturally figure out the purposes of their actions, or their versions of jokes and games (which are in most cases extremely hostile behaviour by the uncivilized). For safety reasons, the uncivilized need to know that they have to explain the purposes of their actions or intended actions properly to the civilized. This requirement will eliminate unsafe hostile assumptions by the uncivilized. The uncivilized need to understand that because they know the civilized because of their supernatural powers and senses, does not necessarily mean that the civilized knows them or want to know them. The uncivilized and their self-destructive nature, regarding their persecution of the civilized, are in the habit of cutting off their noses to spite their faces. The market has been flooded with law books, by the uncivilized pretending to be civilized, with the deliberate wrong interpretation of the constitution of the United Kingdom. Too much quantity and absolutely no quality .They are making it completely impossible for the civilized to have a voice. They do not represent the interest of the civilized or speak for the civilized. The standards used to determine the acceptability or marketability of a book will be that of the uncivilized masquerading as the civilized. As well as the deception of the uncivilized with the wrong interpretation of the constitution, and the culture of hatred that has been spread all around the world as a consequence, they can make you believe a lie or live a lie for decades .An example is the way they hid their uncivilized nature from me, while at the same time misusing their supernatural powers and senses to harm me mentally and physically and breaching the peace and blaming their actions on something else. The wrong interpretation of the constitution of the United Kingdom is a conspiracy involving, Parliament, the judiciary, the police forces, the prison service, the National Health Service at the expense of the mental and physical wellbeing of the civilized and peace and security. When you have this level of criminal activity, who do you turn to for moral guidance, peace and security, law and order? How do you comfort children that experience hopelessness all the days of their lives? What do you say to children whose development has been compromised by these very serious levels of lawlessness? Children will prefer to feel secure with the correct identification and prosecution of criminal activities than playing games of cops and robbers .It is impossible to reason with the uncivilized engaged in this level of criminal activity that is why the force of punishment was incorporated into the constitution of the United Kingdom. As a consequence of the unlawful interpretation of the law by the uncivilized, the civilized are easy prey for the uncivilized. Access to basic services for the civilized is extremely hostile, because of the misuse of supernatural powers and senses by the uncivilized. They are aware of the constitutional rights of the civilized, and see it as a challenge to undermine the civilized with almost every contact. Without the correct interpretation and application of the constitution of the United Kingdom, life will be impossible for the civilized. The only chance of getting through the day, for the civilized, is to avoid or limit contact with the uncivilized. The plan I believe is to compromise the civil nature of the civilized, to make the civilized feel inadequate, so that we will want to have our civil nature altered, so that the uncivilized can create a lawless world unchallenged. This level of attack by the uncivilized was always a one way plan, no retreat no surrender, because you can never expect to repair this level of mental and physical damage to the civilized, regarding the relationship between the civilized and uncivilized .The alarming thing is that some of the uncivilized think that the misuse of their supernatural powers and senses to harm the civilized mentally and physically or to breach the peace in civilized society are jokes and games. What the uncivilized have managed to do is that, they have created, contrary to the constitution, the early stages of hell on earth. They have misused their supernatural powers and senses to achieve this , with their unlawful interpretation of the constitution , you will be judged for your actions, and if you behaved appropriately you will go to their idea of heaven , and if you behave inappropriately you will go to hell .Apart from the fact that their ideas of heaven and hell are both hell , the unlawful creation of their ideas of right and wrong , means that you will never do the right thing, you will always fall below the required standard necessary to go to their idea of heaven , if you are of an uncivilized constitution . The problems they are encountering with their wicked plan, is the civilized. The civilized are the law, with the constitutional rights as law enforcement officers, under the real interpretation of the constitution, the real conditions and the truth must be revealed so that everyone has a chance at a good life. The revelation of the real interpretations of the instructions of the constitution is a must, because of the consequences to those amongst the uncivilized that misuse their supernatural powers and senses to harm the civilized mentally and physically. The uncivilized are aware that the punishment for harming the civilized with the misuse of their supernatural powers and senses is a type of hell they dare not comprehend. Life is such a delicate thing that both the civilized and the uncivilized should not be subjected to horrific living conditions if it can be avoided, even more so the civilized. According to the guidance of the correct interpretation of the constitution of the United Kingdom , the relevant primary areas of law are, civil rights law or constitutional law and criminal law , every other current area of law are either secondary or irrelevant .According to the guidance of the correct interpretation of the constitution , any situation the civilized are in , given the differences in the nature of the civilized and the uncivilized ,the civilized are in that situation in good faith. According to the guidance of the constitution, because the civilized are in any situation in good faith, it is the responsibility of the uncivilized in that situation to make sure the situation is not hostile .The uncivilized cannot claim to be in that situation in good faith, because their supernatural powers and senses will make them aware of what might or might not happen in that situation. It will be criminally negligent of the uncivilized to make that situation develop into a hostile one. The punishment for, and the definition of, criminal behaviour or activity, according to the guidance of the correct interpretation of the constitution is different from the current illegal definition and punishment of criminal behaviour or activity by the uncivilized. The problem the uncivilized will encounter with their attempts to compromise the civil nature of the civilized is the constitution's interpretation of good faith, given the civil nature of the civilized and the constitution's interpretation of criminal negligence given the uncivilized nature of the uncivilized. The problem the uncivilized will encounter with establishing consent of the civilized to the abusive actions of the uncivilized is the constitution's guidance on unhealthy conditions for the civilized. The uncivilized are in the habit of making excuses for their abusive behaviour towards the civilized, they try to make out that the civilized like being persecuted by them .The correct interpretation of having faith in the Christian teachings, is not meant for the civilized but the uncivilized, they are being told not to try to understand the reason behind the guidelines of the constitution on how to behave appropriately when in direct or indirect contact with the civilized. They will not fully understand it because they are not of a civilized nature. It is amazing that the United Kingdom are at the forefront of condemning military dictatorships around the world ,this is a perfect example of the requirement ,to practice what you preach . The uncivilized according to the correct interpretation of the constitution represents military dictatorships, when they rule contrary to the guidance of the constitution, in place of the civilized. The constitution of the United Kingdom has already elected the civilized as the rightful rulers of this planet. So when the uncivilized try to hide behind, consent of the civilized or their version of jokes and games, to persecute the civilized, they should always be aware of the guidelines of the constitution, regarding direct or indirect contact with the civilized. The uncivilized are asking for too much of the inhabitants of this planet and the planet with their blatant disrespect for the sacred instructions of the constitution.

2. HERESY AND THE UNCIVILIZED.

Heresy is when an individual or a group of people advocate changes to a set way of doing things, and these changes are contrary to the constitution, contrary to a constitution meant to provide or provides abundance of goods and services and peace and security, even more so, when these changes are enforced by the misuse of supernatural powers and senses. The changes to the constitution enforced by the misuse of supernatural powers and senses of the uncivilized are meant to create lawlessness, dependency, oppression or domination of the weak by the strong, death, illnesses, ageing whether you have been good or bad, contrary to the constitution. This has created situations that require the weak to worship the strong; the weak are made to become slaves to the barbarism of the strong. There are a lot of different ways that the civilized are being persecuted by the uncivilized .The uncivilized pretend to be civilized with the specific intention of denying the civilized the civil right to govern, contrary to the constitution of the United Kingdom. The uncivilized pretend to be civilized to misuse their supernatural powers and senses to create problems and then blame it on something else. The uncivilized, deliberately creating horrific living conditions to make the civilized live in constant fear .In order to continue with these unconstitutional practices , they ,the uncivilized, interfere supernaturally with the civilized , to give the mysterious impression that the victims of serious persecution , the civilized , are somehow happy or going along with (consenting) being persecuted .This is why the guidance of the constitution confirms that , under no circumstances are the uncivilized to misuse their supernatural powers and senses to harm the civilized mentally or physically ,even if the uncivilized think they are joking or playing games .The uncivilized amongst themselves are aware of the importance of a constitution, order. As much as they try to do the impossible , to change the law to create a lawless society , amongst themselves they still need order to have a bit of organization to carry out their plans .That is a form of constitution, they need some form of order , law (constitution) to get through a day amongst themselves . The lesson for them, even from the process of a revolution, is that they will always need a constitution, to carry out the revolution. So that should be enough for them to understand the impossibility of their situation. So the proof of the impossibility of their situation is that, they need the thing they want to destroy as a tool to destroy it ,and they then need it after it has been destroyed to live amongst themselves either in peace or in organized anarchy . So the proper question to put to them is .What is the point? There really is nothing to gain from it. It only proves the brilliance and sacred nature of this planet, and its constitution. The civilized, according to the constitution, have dominion over this planet. We do not restrict access to what is ours by right, air, water, fruits, land. If there are any restrictions it is because of the wickedness of the uncivilized. The uncivilized are the ones illegally restricting access to these natural resources. The civilized are by nature not intrusive, we will not interfere with what you do or want to do, as long as it does not breach the peace or cause harm to anyone. It really is heresy for the uncivilized to directly or indirectly restrict access to the civilized of what has been instructed by the constitution as belonging to the civilized by right. They are not even allowed to do that to the uncivilized, even more so, the civilized. According to the instructions of the constitution, the civilized should not be restricted from access to goods and services, because of how much it cost. This means that in line with the interpretation of the instructions of the constitution, the civilized should always have enough money to afford to buy what we want, when we want it. It is better to have money and not need it, than to need money and not have it. The uncivilized have deliberately created problems with access to goods and services, with safety of the environment, with health safety etc. In order to make slaves of the civilized to their supernatural powers and senses and to dominate, oppress the civilized, contrary to the instructions of the constitution. The constitution does not allow for the strong to oppress or dominate the weak .This principle is enshrined in the constitution, with the clear instruction that the civilized have dominion over this planet. And to deviate from these instructions will lead to conflict, lawlessness (hell on earth). With these restrictions and impossible living conditions in place created by the misuse of supernatural powers and senses by the uncivilized , unhealthy or unfair concepts like the financial markets , fortune telling , illnesses , ageing , death ,politics , praying (worship) are created to oppress or dominate the civilized , contrary to the constitution. The first reference to death , illness , ageing in the constitution was regarding the punishments of the uncivilized when they misuse their supernatural powers and senses to harm mentally or physically the civilized or to breach the peace in a civilized society. The problem the world is facing at present is its enslavement to the dictates of the uncivilized, contrary to the constitution. Every sacred infrastructure has been destroyed because of trying to create things for the uncivilized to do .It is not necessarily a bad thing to want to look for something interesting to do , but when it involves setting up pointless government departments , the intrusion into people's lives , the breach of the peace , catering to the intoxication of the uncivilized by power regarding their madness to want to always interfere with private decisions people make for themselves or to influence a private plan of an individual , instigated by their intrusive uncivilized nature , it becomes a serious health hazard for the civilized , that will always be easy prey for these types of madness. When they create pointless government departments, they will then need to show its importance, which will involve the misuse of their supernatural powers and senses to create problems to show its relevance, and the civilized will always be caught up in the madness. This same principle applies to fortune telling, the stock market, the civilized will be used to show the importance of these things by trying to make us dependent on it. It is only really important to you if you are poor and are vulnerable in some ways. At the same time it gives the false impression of the superiority of the uncivilized, practices expressly forbidden by the constitution. Some of the uncivilized , because their judgements , decisions , including their games and jokes are guided by their uncivilized nature ,they are not aware that what they might consider help for the civilized or jokes and games are extremely hostile and serious health hazards to the civilized. Trading is not necessarily a bad thing, the question given what is possible, is. What is its purpose? Is it meant to assist or enslave the civilized? The answer to the question is the way to determine the safety of a service or product. The constitution confirms that the civilized cannot possibility commit crimes, because the civilized do not have supernatural powers and senses. The only possible offenders are the uncivilized because of their supernatural powers and senses .This is because of the possible misuse of these supernatural powers and senses to harm mentally or physically the civilized, and the uncivilized, and to breach the peace in a civilized society. Also according to the guidelines of current policing that is operating outside the constitution of the United Kingdom, the code of practice of police officers, under the Police and criminal evidence Act 1984 and its amendment the Criminal procedure and investigations Act 1996, the police are required to use reasonable force while making an arrest. The problem with this is that the differences in the nature of the civilized and the uncivilized make the arrest of the civilized impossible, because the differences are massive, any sort of contact cannot fall within reasonable force. The current evidence of the collective conspiracy of the uncivilized to persecute the civilized does not help. The decisions or judgements of the uncivilized are guided by their uncivilized nature, including their versions of jokes and games, which make them threatening or hazardous to the civilized or to a civilized society. The mental or psychological problems of the civilized , are as a result of being victims of the misuse of supernatural powers and senses or being exposed to or witnesses of the misuse of supernatural powers and senses to breach the peace in a civilized society .It is not going to be resolved by making pointless or meaningless approaches to the civilized under the guise of being concerned for our health for problems they are a party to , but to resolve the problems from its source , which will also include the correct interpretation of the constitution of the United Kingdom. Because such approaches will do more harm than good, because the civilized will be forced into a traumatic, unnecessary contact with those responsible for the problem. The uncivilized, wrongly believe that because the civilized do not say no or yes the same way the uncivilized do, it is mistaken to be an invitation or rejection depending on the circumstances. The civilized are not naturally hostile, so the uncivilized think that our rejections of their abusive practices are not serious. Given the unhealthy effect on the civilized, the rejection is more serious than that of the uncivilized, regardless of appearances. The rejections are only taken seriously, when reinforced by the unsolicited assistance of the uncivilized. This could also be a collective conspiracy of the uncivilized, to undermine directly or indirectly the constitutional authority of the civilized .You will never get policing right, if policing is done on the wrong identification, interpretation and application of the constitution of the United Kingdom. Policing based on the wrong interpretation of the constitution, actually does more harm than good. When a way of life has been engineered with the misuse of supernatural powers and senses, to be founded on the wrong identification, interpretation and application of the constitution, which does serious harm to people, people will still find it difficult to readjust to life under the correct identification, interpretation and application of the constitution, even when it becomes clear that there will be a massive improvement to their standard of living. This reinforces a clear instruction of the constitution, never to start any wrongdoing. Because, it might prove impossible to correct it. There are three ways the uncivilized are deceiving the civilized, in order to deny the civilized our civil rights and at the same time continue with the wrong identification, interpretation and application of the constitution of the United Kingdom. The first way the civilized are being misled, is when the uncivilized pretend to be civilized and are indulging in practices that are an abomination that breeds lawlessness. The second way is the misuse of their supernatural powers and senses to interfere directly with the judgements or the decisions of the civilized, which I will refer to as direct hypnosis. The third way is what I will refer to as indirect hypnosis, involving the uncivilized conspiring collectively to make the civilized witness unlawful practices, to make the civilized believe that those practices are lawful. This conspiracy collectively involves the deliberate compromise of the only source of knowledge for the civilized, education. The guidance of the constitution of the United Kingdom , originating from where civil rights were formulated in the garden of Eden in the Christian teachings , does not forbid the civilized from obtaining knowledge . What is forbidden is the way the knowledge is obtained. It is a clear instruction to the uncivilized not to compromise the civil nature of the civilized. This means that they are not allowed to compromise the civil nature of the civilized by misusing their supernatural powers and senses to give the civilized supernatural powers and senses. The civilized in the Garden of Eden, were initially educated or given knowledge through education not to eat the forbidden fruit in the Garden of Eden. This was a direct instruction to the uncivilized not to compromise the civil nature of the civilized. The real purpose of socialism, created by the uncivilized, socialists that are referred to as reds, is to misuse their supernatural powers and senses to violate the civil rights of the civilized, to compromise permanently the civil nature of the civilized or to breach the peace in a civilized society, in order to create lawlessness (hell on earth), contrary to the constitution. If your civil nature is compromised, you automatically lose your individual rights (civil rights), and then you will be exposed to unchallenged attacks on you by the uncivilized. So it is quite clear , why the uncivilized keep sabotaging the interests of the civilized like films , music , books etc. ,in order to communicate supernaturally to the civilized , contrary to the instructions of the constitution , with the intention of compromising the civil nature of the civilized. The civilized are being tempted by this unlawful interference by the uncivilized, which will eventually lead to the altering of the civil nature of the civilized. They are of the opinion that they can create an infrastructure in hell, contrary to the guidance of the constitution. Socialism, which is politics generally, represents all the burdens of a relationship without any benefits for the civilized. It represents the loss of civil rights for the civilized, and encourages the illegal, immoral delusion of the uncivilized to continue with the illegal persecution of the civilized. Their actions, confirms them, according to the guidelines of the constitution, as enemies of the civilized. They have introduced an unconstitutional practice, politics, to make the civilized dependent on those the constitution defines as enemies of the civilized. According to the constitution socialism can only operate illegally, this means it represents lawlessness, and the unconstitutional persecution of the civilized. The demonic practices of interfering in someone else's life , their decisions , their independence in direct or indirect ways by the barbarism of the uncivilized ,is the purpose of misleading , misinforming or miseducating the young and the vulnerable , that illness , death , ageing is part of the natural course of life ,it makes no difference if you are good or bad , contrary to the instructions of the constitution. The uncivilized are trying to make legitimate the unlawful interference in your life. Regardless of your views on life the uncivilized do not have the right to kill you, make you ill, make you age after a you become an adult .Death, ageing, illness, poverty are punishments meant for the uncivilized that misuse their supernatural powers and senses to harm mentally or physically the civilized, or the uncivilized or to breach the peace in a civilized society. My experiences so far of the practices of the uncivilized , is that they are intoxicated by power and have a God complex .And as a consequence they are easily susceptible to peer pressure to persecute the civilized as a collective , through their actions or inactions . Given the magnitude of the abomination of the practices of the uncivilized as a collective, they should be treated in a similar way to recovering alcoholics with regard to their supernatural powers and senses and trying to make decisions directly or indirectly about the lives of other people. Allowing them to vote is similar to giving a recovering alcoholic alcohol. This includes altering the normal functions of television, films, radio, music, so that they can communicate supernaturally directly or indirectly with someone watching films or listening to music .All the burdens of a relationship with nothing to gain for the civilized, it is extremely hazardous to the civilized and the altered functions unconstitutional. Because of the uncivilized nature of the uncivilized , they deliberately set out , unprovoked , to create hostile conditions ,relationships , conversations , contacts , because it caters to their uncivilized nature at the expense of the physical and mental wellbeing of the civilized and the peace and security in a civilized society. The provision of goods and services can be achieved with the proper use of their supernatural powers and senses, with little or no effort, and with little or no contact with them. But they always opt for contact and a lot of unnecessary effort with doing things, even with situations that nature has made easier to access things with little or no effort, they wreck it, and make it more difficult to have access to these things .So that they can create hostile conditions. When these problems that they deliberately created start having an adverse effect on them, they try to blame the intended victims, the civilized. It is for the civilized to decide who we want to have personal relationships with or contact, it is not for the uncivilized to try to force these things on the civilized with the misuse of their supernatural powers and senses. According to the instructions of the constitution of the United Kingdom, the civilized as senior law enforcement officers, should be in receipt of salaries that acknowledges those sacred senior official positions. This is apart from a legal confirmation by the constitution, giving ownership to the civilized of all natural resources, land, water, air etc. The salary of a senior law enforcement officer is meant to be symbolic .The civilized are not technically paid, because you cannot pay someone with something that already belongs to them. If anything is left to the goodwill of the uncivilized, it will never get done, you will wait indefinitely. So when they try to interfere with the independence of the civilized, so that the civilized will then be dependent on the non-existent goodwill of the uncivilized, it is an indirect declaration of war on the civilized by the uncivilized. In science fiction films like star trek , the principle of replication , found on trees with fruits has been developed to include ready-made food on replicator machines .This is very possible , it is more hygienic , requires little or no effort. So the question is why the pointless delays to do what is right? The uncivilized have developed in desperation, the principle of retaliation, the civilized as the victims of their retaliation, when the constitution confirms that the civilized can do no wrong. It is a desperate concept that they think will lead to the real plan to try to compromise the civil nature of the civilized. They cannot accept the truth, according to the instructions of the constitution that the civilized are actually civilized in the same way as defined in the Garden of Eden, and are their superiors, contrary to the misconception fuelled by the uncivilized. Contrary to the deliberate misinterpretation of the constitution, by the uncivilized declaring themselves gods, because of their supernatural powers and senses. The only reference directly or indirectly to the word gods or god, by the instructor (creator), has been in reference to the civilized and not the uncivilized.

3. THE MISCONCEPTION THAT THE UNCIVILIZED ARE GODS CONTRARY TO THE LAW.

The uncivilized, believe that their supernatural powers and senses makes them gods, contrary to the guidance of the constitution. They are of the mistaken belief that their supernatural powers and senses means that they are above the law. The point of a constitution is because of the possible problems associated with the possible misuse of supernatural powers and senses amongst the uncivilized, to the civilized and to peace and security in a civilized society. Part of the development of the civilized and uncivilized has been filled with stories of gods in certain civilizations , and they were always quick to point out that what made them gods and superior to the civilized ,which was always expressed and implied, is their supernatural powers and senses. And how these gods needed to be worshipped in order for them to be happy, and you to be in their favour. The civilized have been made slaves to the needs of the uncivilized to be worshipped. It will always require the constant flow of problems in the lives of the civilized, to maintain the need to worship the uncivilized. They deliberately interfere supernaturally with the private decisions of the civilized, not for any legitimate, goodwill purpose, but to impose their ideas on the civilized by force, because they are intoxicated by power. For the civilized to have what should be an informal conversation with the uncivilized , is extremely hazardous because , their views on any subject obtained from an informal conversation , will directly or indirectly be forced on the civilized, whether you are agree with their ideas or not , whether those ideas are unhealthy or not for the civilized . This enforces their objectives to dominate or oppress the civilized. This horrific behaviour of the uncivilized towards the civilized is because of their mistaken beliefs that they are superior to the civilized, which makes them gods, and should be worshipped by the civilized. They interfere with the plans of the civilized or plan the lives of the civilized, just to do it, rather than it serving any useful purpose to the civilized. It is because the uncivilized are of the mistaken belief that they are gods , that is why they always want to plan the lives of the civilized with the use of their supernatural powers and senses ,whether invited to do it or not , whether there is a need for it or not . They go as far as interfering with the judgements, and decisions of the civilized, with the misuse of their supernatural powers and senses, to give the impression that the civilized are not competent enough to take care of ourselves. They try to achieve this objective directly with the misuse of their supernatural powers and senses or indirectly by compromising the only source of knowledge for the civilized, education. This also includes the deliberate interference with the financial security of the civilized, given the nature of the world. This establishes a pattern of destructive behaviour by the uncivilized towards the civilized. It has not occurred to the uncivilized , that since the constitution confirms that the civilized are naturally incapable of doing wrong, because of our civil nature, to impose some further unconstitutional rules on the civilized requiring more unnecessary restrictions on us , is extremely hostile and seriously unhealthy. They want to believe that these unnecessary enforced restrictions on the civilized are their versions of jokes and games. The problem is this god complex thing about the uncivilized and they see the civilized as an opportunity to live out their self-destructive beliefs that they are gods because of their supernatural powers and senses. According to the Christian principles, the constitution, every reference to God, has been that God is extremely good and wants the best for everyone. This implies that since God is very good, given the differences in their uncivilized nature and the civil nature of the civilized, means that to be good means to be civilized, which means that God is of a civil nature, no supernatural powers and senses. This means that the creator's reference to God was with regard to Adam, and later Jesus Christ. This means that God is the son of the creator. Because of the constitution's implied and expressed guidance that God is good , and to be good , means to be civilized .Based on this principle , was how the nobility that represents the civilized and the commoners or peasants that represents the uncivilized was founded. Contrary to the constitution , the uncivilized consider themselves gods, at the expense of the physical and mental wellbeing of the civilized .The constitution , which is the Christian principles ,civil rights , condemns the misuse of supernatural powers and senses to harm the civilized , mentally or physically , or to breach the peace in a civilized society. The uncivilized wrongly believe that their supernatural powers and senses make them gods, contrary to the guidance of the constitution. And it is because of this misguided belief, that the uncivilized think that they can misuse their supernatural powers and senses to harm the civilized, mentally or physically and to breach the peace in a civilized society. According to the guidance of the constitution, everything on this planet belongs to the civilized, and the civilized by our nature allow free access to what are ours by right (water, air, fruits, and natural resources). If there are any alterations to these principles of access, it is not the fault of the civilized, but because of the wickedness of the uncivilized. The uncivilized have deliberately set out to make a mess of the lives of the civilized, in order to give the false impression that they have better lives than the civilized; this helps them maintain the delusion that they are gods, contrary to the guidance of the constitution. Given the differences in the uncivilized nature of the uncivilized and the nature of the civilized, it is impossible for the uncivilized to interpret any of the actions of the civilized as hostile, so the magnitude of the hostility towards the civilized by the uncivilized is illogical. Given the god complex attitude of the uncivilized towards the civilized, it is extremely dangerous for the civilized to have any sort of contact with the uncivilized. The uncivilized, as a consequence of their hostility towards the civilized have no interpersonal skills, so it is pointless for the uncivilized to initiate direct or indirect contact with the civilized. The god complex of the uncivilized, which has proven to be a serious threat to international peace and security, as well as a serious threat to the mental and physical wellbeing of the civilized, continues to prove a serious nightmare for peace and security and the safety of the civilized, because of the continued efforts of the uncivilized to make the civilized dependent on them. This is also a guilty response of the uncivilized to their past deeds , because once the instructions of the constitution are implemented in full , it will reveal that the civilized do not actually need the uncivilized , rather the uncivilized will always need the peace and security that the civilized will provide . Because once the novelty of their lust for barbarism diminishes, they will be in serious need for the shelter of law and order. The added assault on the civilized by the barbarism of the uncivilized, is that, once they get tired of what they had conspired to do, to make the civilized dependent on them unnecessarily, they will try to claim that the civilized are a burden. The purpose of the law is to regulate the use of supernatural powers and senses by the uncivilized, to prevent them from being intoxicated by their powers and as a consequence create hell on earth. The purpose of the law is to help the uncivilized understand when they have descended into complete madness, by being intoxicated by their supernatural powers and senses. Because of the god complex of the uncivilized, they believe wrongly that they have the right to invade the privacy of the civilized, with the intention of communicating supernaturally, directly or indirectly with the civilized, for one misguided purpose after another, contrary to the guidance of the constitution. This delusion has made them misuse their supernatural powers and senses to plan the lives of the civilized, creating accidents and the civilized as victims injured physically or mentally, they do these things as forms of punishments for the civilized. That they believe have fallen short of their illegal versions of right and wrong. According to their unconstitutional versions of right and wrong, for the civilized to fall below their set standards, is when the civilized reject their abusive (criminal) behaviour. In order to impose their illegal interpretation of the constitution , on the civilized , about the uncivilized being gods , they misuse their supernatural powers and senses to interfere with the self-confidence of the civilized , to make the civilized have very low self-esteem , in order to dominate the civilized in more ways than one . This includes the misuse of their supernatural powers and senses to alter the physical appearance of the civilized, in different ways, to undermine our self-confidence. These attacks are done with very serious bad intentions that they try to disguise as jokes and games. The guidance of the constitution does not interpret those serious attacks on the civilized as jokes and games. And the effects of those serious attacks on the health of the civilized can never be interpreted by any reasonable person as jokes and games. They try to get involved in private decisions the civilized try to make, which will certainly involve unhealthy dramatics, false show of concern for the wellbeing of the civilized, by the uncivilized to divert attention from the main conspiracy of the uncivilized, which is the continuation of the persecution of the civilized. In order to continue with the illegal persecution of the civilized, they misuse their supernatural powers and senses, to interfere with the civilized supernaturally, a form of mind and physical control, to give the false impression that the civilized are willing participants of our persecution. The uncivilized try to force some relationships on the civilized in indirect ways, by making too much of a brief encounter, with the uncivilized, which is really unavoidable, so that if they cannot find faults in you directly, they try to find faults through your association with the uncivilized. This practice by the uncivilized is unconstitutional. It is the desperation of the uncivilized to undermine the civilized, in order to continue being seen as gods, contrary to the constitution.

4. THE GAMES OF THE UNCIVILIZED.

What the uncivilized consider to be games are extremely hostile (hazardous) to the civilized. The uncivilized nature of the uncivilized makes their judgements and decisions, including their jokes and games, which are influenced by their uncivilized nature, extremely hostile to the civilized, and a threat to international peace and security. Something that starts off as a joke or game concludes with them trying to kill each other. This barbarism of the uncivilized is reflected in every conversation they try to initiate , the contents are always extremely hostile , which they will consider to be jokes and games , which will then deteriorate into a life threatening situation for the civilized , that cannot naturally interpret such serious hostilities as jokes and games . For the civilized, we are either slaves to the barbarism of the uncivilized, which is a living hell for the civilized, or we will be persecuted for rejecting the barbarism of the uncivilized, collectively by the uncivilized, which becomes a living hell for the civilized, contrary to the guidance of the constitution. Most of the time the hostilities are subtle but extremely threatening and hazardous , especially amongst the white race ,that try to initiate contact directly or indirectly with the civilized, by trying to pretend to be of a civilized nature , and using the pretence to harm mentally and physically the civilized. When their abusive actions are rejected by the civilized we are illegally labelled as severely mentally impaired or criminals. Even those amongst the uncivilized that refer to themselves as Angels, engage in the barbarism of misinforming, misleading the civilized and the young of the uncivilized. So that they can engage in and enjoy the hunting sport of misusing their supernatural powers and senses to harm mentally and physically the civilized, in the process of correcting the unintentional bad practices brought about by the deliberate compromise of the education of the civilized, that should not have been allowed to develop through the deliberate miseducation of the civilized. With this in mind they cannot be allowed to be referred to as Angels, given what that has been presented to signify, rather they should be referred to as demons. Also the labelling of some of the uncivilized as Angels is dangerous for the civilized, because the uncivilized are of the mistaken belief that being labelled Angels gives them the right to interfere supernaturally with the civilized. They can then make self-destructive assumptions that they have something to hide behind that makes their unlawful attacks on the civilized, legitimate. Their actions towards the civilized, is similar to breeding animals for the purpose of hunting and killing these animals. According to the guidance of the constitution, the uncivilized are not allowed to misuse their supernatural powers and senses to harm mentally or physically the civilized or to breach the peace in a civilized society, even if the uncivilized think they are joking or playing games. Contrary to the misconception created by the uncivilized , it is actually the civilized that are capable of identifying the angels and demons amongst the uncivilized , given what they try to present or interpret as angels or demons .These same criminals , given the gravity or magnitude of their criminal activities think they can take the moral high ground , by deceiving those they consider vulnerable , into believing that their demonic practices aimed at the deliberate persecution of the civilized , is an unconstitutional method of assessing or educating the civilized. As constitutional law enforcement officers, the civilized cannot allow such delusions, in the interest of law and order. Such delusions compromise the development of the young, and undermine their security. My judgement is not emotionally driven (not motivated by revenge); it is logical, consistent with the guidelines of the constitution. This is why the civilized are by nature, given the differences in the nature of the uncivilized and the civilized, commissioners of police, because policing has to be consistent with the guidelines of the real   constitution of the United Kingdom. The civilized are charged with commissioning a real police force, for the purposes of real policing that is consistent with the guidelines of the constitution. The uncivilized need to understand that the civilized are constitutional law enforcement officers, of a sacred constitution. Rather than the uncivilized to think they are assessing the civilized, they should know that they the uncivilized are the ones being assessed. The guidance of the constitution, regarding the punishments for the uncivilized that misuse their supernatural powers and senses to harm mentally and physically the civilized or to breach the peace in a civilized society, is very strict. In recognition of the serious dangers associated with the misuse of supernatural powers and senses. The uncivilized cannot be reasoned with, once they develop the habit of misusing their supernatural powers and senses to harm mentally or physically the civilized or to breach the peace in a civilized society .So in order to establish law and order, it has to be done through the force of punishment. The misuse of supernatural powers and senses of the uncivilized, contrary to the strict guidelines of the constitution, in the guise of punishments, to harm mentally or physically the civilized, is political, aimed at undermining the civil rights of the civilized. The uncivilized need to be aware, when they develop the urge to plan the lives of the civilized, that their decisions, including their jokes and games are guided by their uncivilized nature, and could be seriously harmful mentally or physically to the civilized, so they need to seek the consent or approval of the civilized before embarking on any unsolicited course of action. The civilized are not slaves to the barbarism of the uncivilized. The lessons of history regarding the nobility and the working class , the required behaviour when the working class are in the presence of the nobility , is about the exercise of serious self-control with regard to the use of their supernatural powers and senses . My experiences so far confirm that the reason the uncivilized want to initiate contact with the civilized, is to try to oppress or dominate the civilized, with the misuse of their supernatural powers and senses. They also try to do this with their version of jokes and games. I do not see my civil nature as a form of sacrifice, but in order to give the uncivilized an understanding of the seriousness of their hostilities towards the civilized, they can look at the civil nature of the civilized, having no supernatural powers and senses, as a sacrifice for world peace and security. And the civilized should not be made to feel vulnerable as a consequence of this sacrifice, or ridiculed, or made to feel inadequate, or put in harm's way.

I recently self- published a similar small book about the law. I could not find a publisher to publish the book, because the book condemns the collective conspiracy of the uncivilized, including publishers to mislead, misinform people about the correct interpretation of the law, as a consequence creating lawlessness. The books that they publish represent the current practices of show without substance. And also their standards are of those of an uncivilized nature pretending to be civilized. The problems are similar to their stories of Nazi Germany, the impossibility of a persecuted Jew, trying to publish a book about the persecution of Jews in Nazi Germany, by a Nazi publishing company, and the book for a Nazi market. The use of computers is a new experience for me, but the completed manuscript came out a lot better on my computer. I believe that there was some supernatural interference. The uncivilized need to undermine the civilized, including our efforts, to continue illegally to govern.

5. AUTHOR'S NOTES.

This is the second book I have written about what I believe to be the correct identification, interpretation and application of the constitution of the United Kingdom. And the effects on the vulnerable of the wrong interpretation of the law. How the vulnerable are caught in the middle of power struggles, resulting from the wrong identification, interpretation and application of the constitution of the United Kingdom. The evidence of this power struggle is reflected in the composition and protocols in Parliament. I do not want to be a writer, but the uncivilized are making life hell for the civilized. Writing these two small books about the law was very difficult, because it was done under extremely hostile conditions. I have been and continue to be under constant attacks from the uncivilized.

6. AUTHOR'S BIOGRAPHY.

I am of African origin. I was born in the United Kingdom. I am a graduate of an Anglican seminary school. I graduated from the University of East London, with a law degree.

7. BIBLIOGRAPHY.

The bible. The first book of Moses: Genesis.